THE ART OF **THE ICON**

NIGEL CAWTHORNE

BARNES & NOBLE

NEW YORK

Copyright © Octopus Publishing Group
Ltd 1997, 2006

First published in 1997 by Hamlyn,
a division of Octopus Publishing
Group Ltd

This 2006 edition published by Barnes &
Noble, Inc. by arrangement with Bounty
Books, a division of Octopus Publishing
Group Ltd.

Executive Editor: Mike Evans
Editors: Humaira Husain, Sharon Ashman
Art Director: Keith Martin
Executive Art Editor: Mark Winwood
Design: Rozelle Bentheim
Map Illustrator: Peter Gerrish
Production Controller: Louise Hall
Picture Research: Zoë Holtermann

ISBN-13: 978-0-7607-8879-0
ISBN-10: 0-7607-8879-0

A CIP catalogue record for this book is
available from the British Library

Printed and bound in China

1 3 5 7 9 10 8 6 4 2

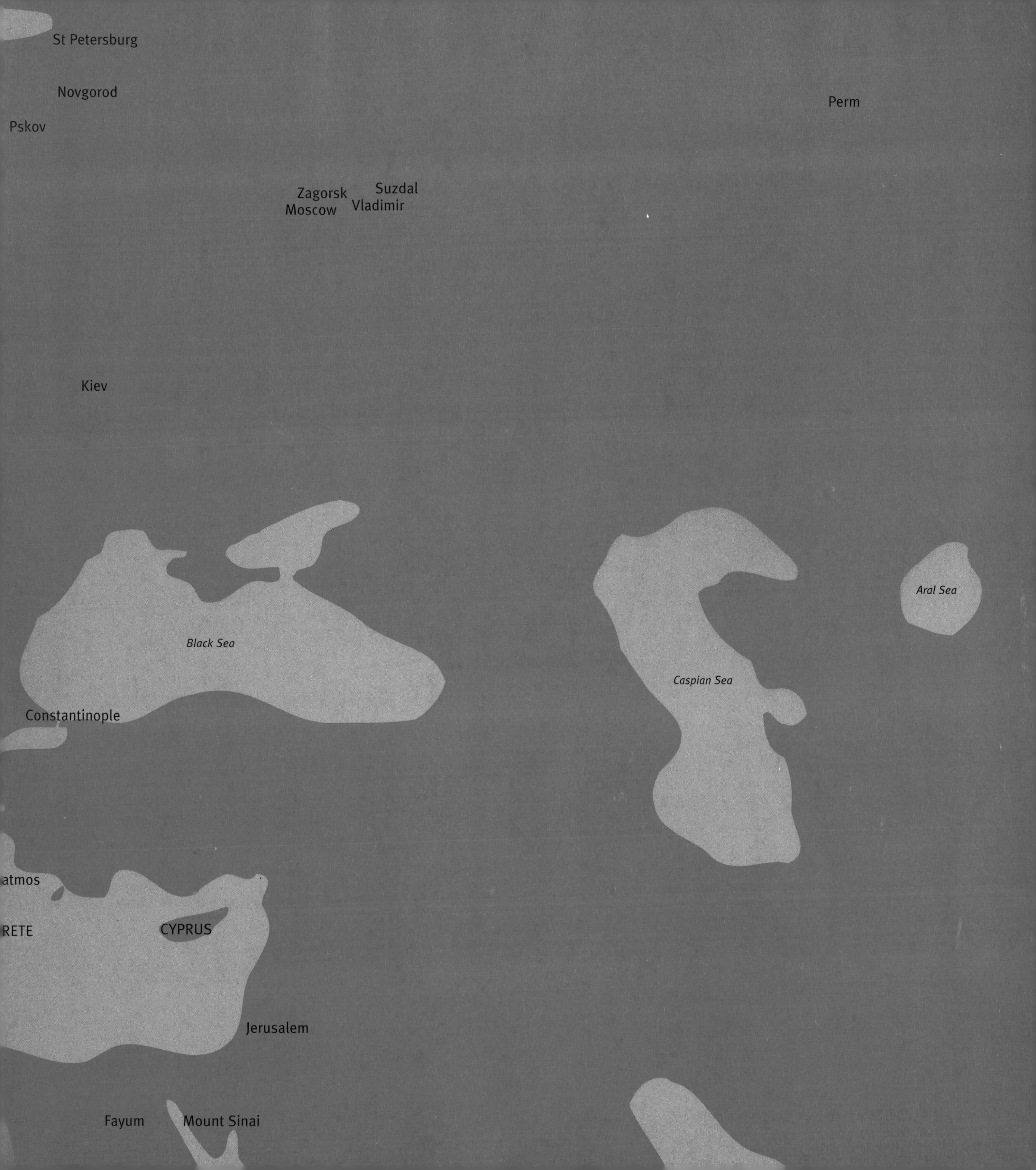

St Petersburg

Novgorod

Pskov

Perm

Zagorsk   Suzdal
Moscow   Vladimir

Kiev

Black Sea

Caspian Sea

Aral Sea

Constantinople

atmos

RETE   CYPRUS

Jerusalem

Fayum   Mount Sinai

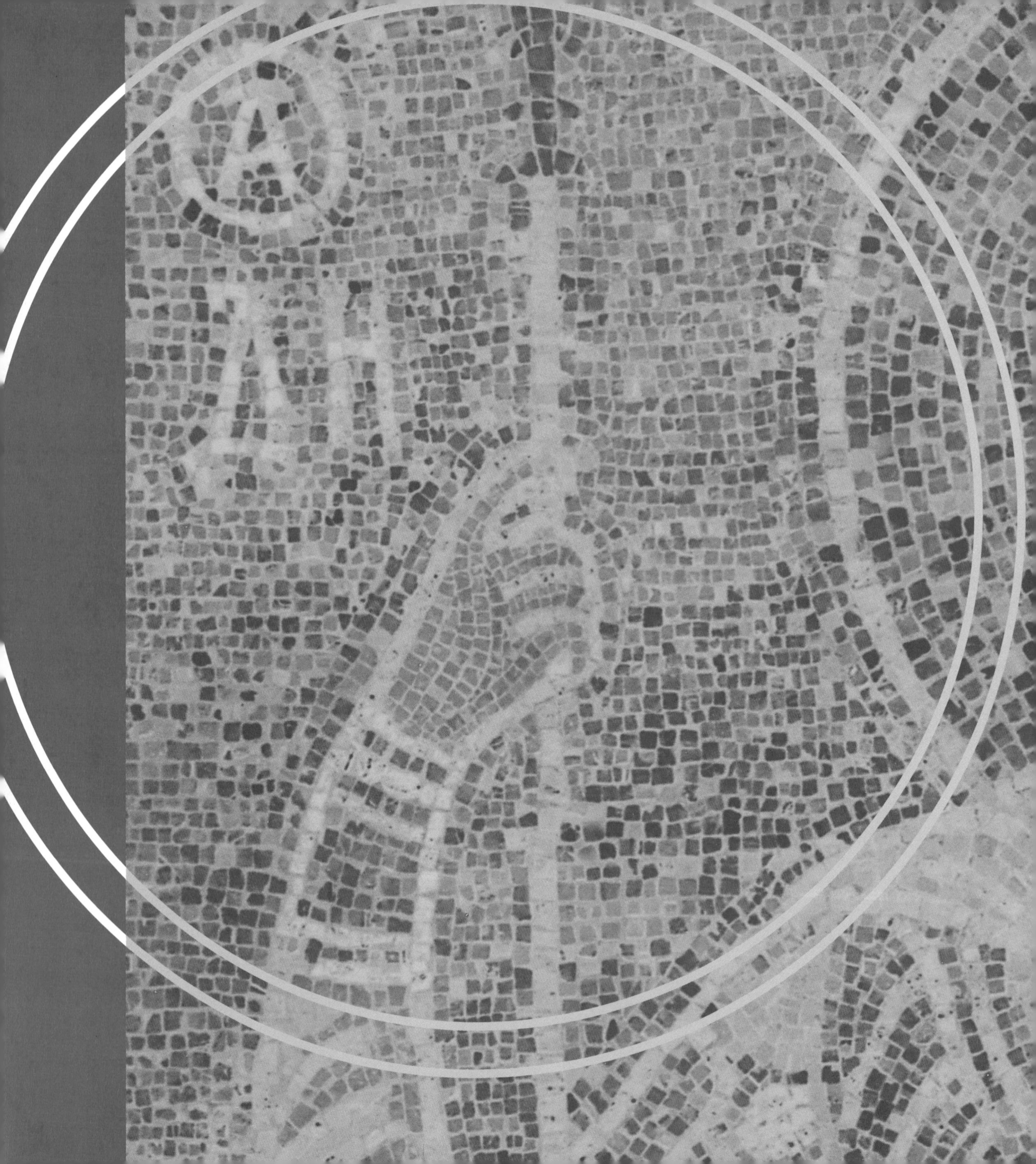

The basic meaning of the word icon is an an image or likeness, but it has come to signify a religious painting. Icons are usually painted by monks and are often thought to have been divinely inspired. They frequently repeat the same subject matter and are rendered in the same style. The original aim of the monastic artists was to remove any sense of individuality, leading to the claim that icons were 'acheiropoieten' – that is, not made by human hand.

Although any religious painting can be termed an icon, the paintings that are generally considered to be 'proper' icons were usually painted on wooden panels. In the Mediterranean, birch, lime, alder and cypress were used, but in Russia, pine was the wood of choice. Russian pine is less resinous than more southerly varieties.

Some icons are flat, but most have the central area of the wood hollowed out, thus creating a raised border or frame around the main portion of the image. The wood was then covered in coarse canvas, which was treated with gesso – plaster of Paris mixed with fine chalk or powdered alabaster to give a white ground for the painting. As many as eight layers of gesso were applied to the canvas, building up a smooth surface for the artist to work on.

The earliest icons were painted using the encaustic process, in which pigments are burnt into the painting using hot wax. By the eighth century, however, egg tempura had taken over, and in the fifteenth century, oil paints were introduced.

The finished work was then varnished, but this absorbed soot and grime, and the colours faded quickly. To prevent this discoloration, the surface of the icon was sometimes shielded by a highly decorated sheet of precious metal, which left only the most important elements of the painting open to view.

The finished icons were then hung on the iconostasis, which is a wooden screen that divides the nave of the church – which symbolizes the earthly realm of man – from the sanctuary – which symbolizes the realm of God. In Russian churches the iconostasis extends all the way to the roof of the church, thus completely separating the sanctuary from the nave.

▶ **Madonna of the Annunciation**
Twelfth-century icon depicting the Virgin Mary, one of the traditional subjects of early icon painters

For their subject matter, icons traditionally concentrate on a limited number of subjects. The earliest icons show only Christ, the Virgin Mary and the leading apostles. The canon was then broadened to include the twelve great feasts of the Christian calendar. These comprise the four feasts of the Mother of God – the Nativity of the Blessed Virgin Mary, the Presentation of Mary in the Temple, the Annunciation and the Dormition of the Mother of God, known as the Assumption in the Western Church – the six feasts of Christ – the Nativity, the Presentation of Jesus in the Temple, the Baptism of Jesus, the Theophany (Manifestation of God), the Entry into Jerusalem and the Ascension – and, finally, Pentecost and the Exaltation of the Cross.

Another celebration depicted on icons is the Feast of Feasts, which is the Resurrection of Christ, or the Descent into Hades. Other feasts also have their own icons, such as the Resurrection of Lazarus, the Crucifixion, the Nativity of John the Baptist and the Last Supper.

The lives of the saints also appear in icons. Very occasionally, other scenes from the Old and New Testaments make an appearance, such as the virtuous ascending to heaven, the Massacre of the Innocents, the Flight into Egypt and the Last Judgment. In addition, by the sixteenth century, icon painters were plundering the Apocrypha and the lives of obscure local saints for artistic inspiration.

▶ **Baptism of Christ**
Late fourteenth-century icon portraying one of the six great feasts of Christ, which were regularly depicted on icons as well as in other religious paintings

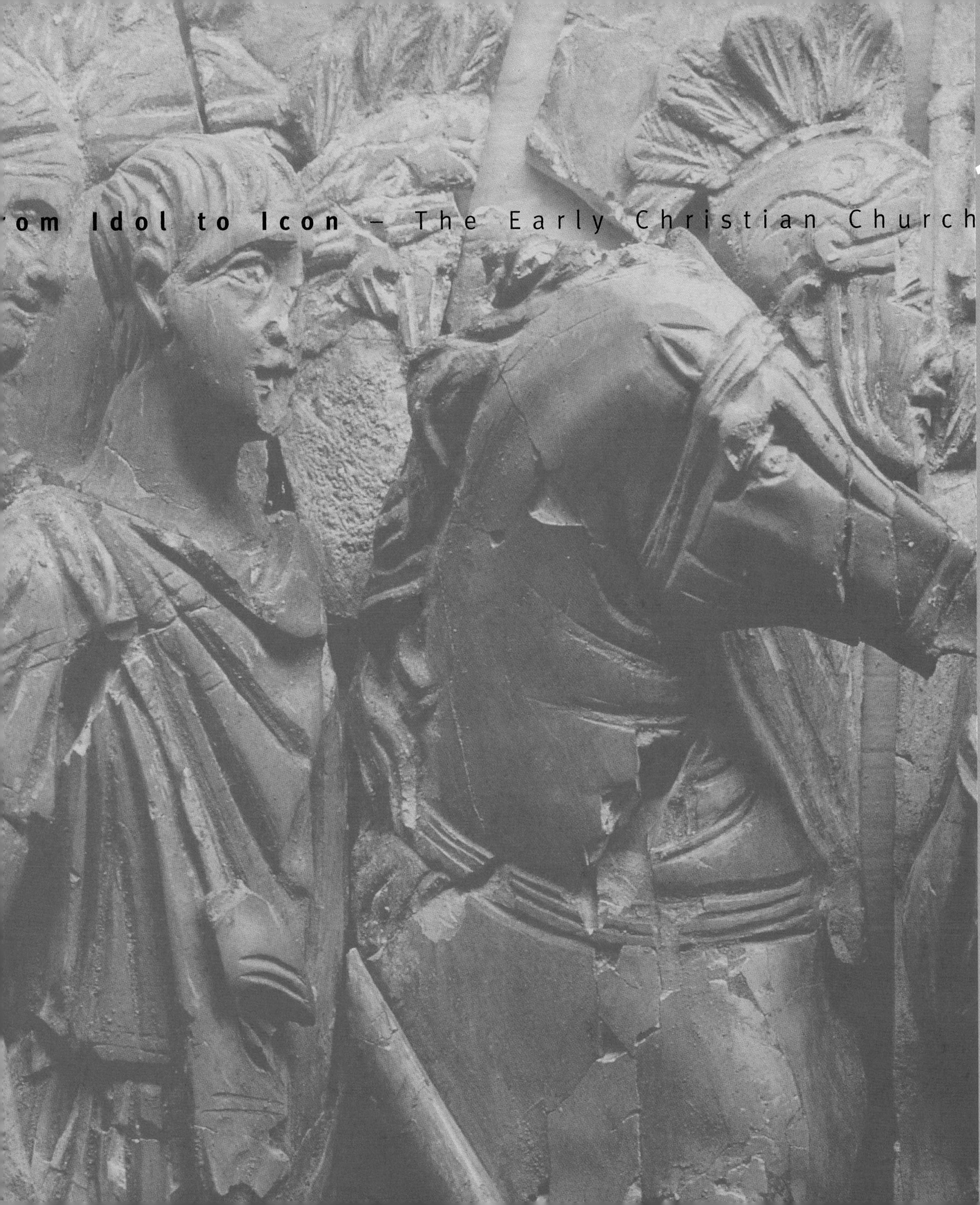

1

rom Idol to Icon – The Early Christian Church

The Third Commandment says: 'Thou shalt not make unto thee any graven image, or any likeness of anything that is in heaven above, or that is in the earth beneath, or that is in the water under the earth: Thou shalt not bow down thyself to them or serve them ...' (Exodus Chapter 20, verses 4 and 5). This could be interpreted as meaning that the making of icons was prohibited by the Bible. Indeed, for Jews that is exactly what it is taken to mean. The Temple in Jerusalem contained no images. Such a thing would have been considered blasphemy.

However, at Dura Europos near Damascus in Syria, there are the ruins of a synagogue and a church, which were destroyed in AD 257, both of which contained images. Remarkably, the synagogue was decorated with episodes from Hebrew scriptures rendered in the flat, linear style used in the pagan temple nearby. The church borrowed that same rigid style in its depiction of Adam and Eve. Yet, when it came to the portrayal of Christ as the Good Shepherd and performing various miracles, the style is a good deal freer and seems to have drawn on a different tradition.

Interestingly, it is in the depiction of Christ that Christian iconography justifies itself. As God had made himself flesh in Christ, it could no longer be considered sacrilege to portray God's existence in the real world. Indeed, Christians came to believe that to depict the real world in art was to celebrate the existence of an invisible God, not to affront him.

One of the most important influences on early icons was the ancient practice of painting memorial pictures. The Egyptians particularly liked to paint pictures of the dead, even when they preserved their mummified remains. Wooden sarcophagi are usually decorated with a painting of the person inside as they would have appeared in life.

The depiction of gods was not forbidden to the Egyptians. Paintings of enthroned gods were found at Fayum. Some of these were triptychs, a familiar device in later Christian icons, especially those in the Russian Orthodox tradition. The Egyptian triptychs portray one god standing in a central panel with panels depicting seated gods flanking it.

The first major outpouring of Christian art appeared in the second and third centuries when Christians began to paint pastoral and elegiac scenes in the catacombs beneath Rome. This underground art was the antithesis of the triumphalist art of Imperial Rome that flourished in the city above. However, it borrowed from the wall paintings seen in Pompeii and also

▲ **St Catherine's Monastery, Mount Sinai**
The monastery, which was built around 520 AD, is home to
an outstanding collection of icons, some of which date
back to early Byzantine times

◄ **Early Christian fresco**
The Christian establishment came to believe that depicting
the real world in art was a celebration of God

◄◄ **Egyptian linen painting**
First-century painting depicting the jackal-
headed god Anubis receiving a new subject
into the Kingdom of the Dead

◄ **Egyptian mummy portraits**
The direct gaze of the subjects in these
second- and third-century portraits bears a
striking similarity to the watchful expression of
the central figures in icon painting

▲ **Roman fresco from Pompeii**
Similarities in painting styles reveal how the various cultures
of the ancient world were influenced by each other's art

from the Greek tradition. A philosopher reading to his pupils was a popular Greek image. In Christian iconography that same image became Christ delivering the Word.

The persecution of early Christians led to the veneration of the martyrs. Their sacrifices provided important subject matter for early icon artists. After the conversion of the Emperor Constantine in the fourth century and the end of persecution, Christian artists adapted this realistic style to portray the deeds of the living. The portraits of the great and the good that had by tradition been hung in Roman homes now became suffused with Christian imagery.

However, as the Christian Church grew, the religious tradition became diluted. Many of the elements of the worship of Mithras, the sun god, were incorporated into Christian art and, it is argued, Mithras was the origin of the halo around the head of Christ and the saints in Christian works.

In Imperial Rome, the image of the emperor had been worshipped. Images of the Christian Constantine, even after Christianity became the state religion, were worshipped in this way. After all, Constantine could now be seen as God's secular representative on Earth. Emperors would appear in diptychs, alongside the images of saints.

As paganism often revolved around worshipping an object or an image, it was a small step for new converts to Christianity to venerate the icon rather than what it portrayed. The veneration of relics, especially of what were thought to be fragments of the True Cross, also prepared the way for the worship of icons in the fourth century.

By the fifth century St Augustine, Epiphanius of Salamis and others mention the cult of icon worship. In the early sixth century, Hypatius of Ephesus makes the first reference to the practice of proskynesis, that is, prostrating oneself before an icon. By the end of the sixth century, many icons were said to have miraculous properties.

Since new Christians came from a multiplicity of pagan backgrounds, the worship of religious relics and icons took a central role in holding the new religion together. However, believers in the older Jewish tradition of an invisible God began to condemn this as idolatry. They became the iconoclasts, the breakers of icons.

Until the eighth century the iconodules – those who favoured icon worship – were in the ascendancy. A mandylion, an image of Christ's face on

▶ **The Roman god Mithras**
Mithras was always shown with a halo, and this symbol was adopted by the Christian Church to signify the concept of divinity in their sacred images

▶▶ **Emperor Constantine the Great**
Constantine, the first Roman emperor to convert to Christianity, was sanctified after his death and thereafter depicted as a saint with a halo

a linen cloth said to have been made by Christ himself, was carried by the Imperial Roman armies fighting the Persians. This, it was believed, had cured King Abgar of Edessa of leprosy and had given the Imperial army victory at Edessa in Turkey in 544. Emperor Heraclius himself paraded it before his troops in 622.

In 626, when the Persians and Avars were besieging Constantinople, the Patriarch ordered that the image of the Madonna and Child be painted on the city gates. It seemed to work. Within a year the enemy fleet had been sunk at the Golden Horn and Heraclius, who carried with him the *Image of Edessa*, had defeated the Persians at Nineveh. The mandylion was taken to Constantinople in 944 and lost in the sack of 1204.

However, the iconodules went too far in ascribing miraculous properties to their icons. When a man banged a nail into an icon of St Peter, it was said that he was struck with a terrible pain in the head until the nail was removed. Another icon was said to exude oil, which a Sardinian nun used for healing. When she asked a priest to move the icon for her, his hand shrivelled up and he died three days later. When she moved it herself, it was said to have grown breasts.

In 726, Emperor Leo III ordered that all icons be removed from churches. This was a political move rather than a religious one, however. Leo had come to power with the support of the armies of Armenia and Anatolia, which lay to the east and were vital to protect the empire from the onslaught of Islam, and the Armenians and Anatolians were traditionally iconoclasts. As a result of the ban, the Italian Church under Pope Gregory II seceded from the empire.

Leo's son Constantine V stepped up the crusade against the iconodules. In 754, he banned the manufacture, possession and worship of icons. The great monasteries were closed and the monks who produced icons arrested. Some were paraded in the Hippodrome alongside prostitutes and forced to marry them. Many monks died in prison. The destruction was so complete that we now know very little about icon painting from this early period. However, some early icons were hidden in the monastery of St Catherine on Mount Sinai. Four were discovered there by the Russian priest Porphyrius Uspensky and taken to Kiev in the middle of the nineteenth century. Since then, other early icons have been found concealed in St Catherine's monastery.

▶ **Mandylion icon**

Such images of Christ's face imprinted on linen cloth were believed to have been made by Christ himself

▲ **Monastery of St Catherine, Mount Sinai**
The sanctuary for icons threatened in the eighth century, the monastery was sited beneath the mountain top where Moses was believed to have received the Ten Commandments

In 786, when the Empress Irene, widow of the iconoclast Leo IV, tried to restore the worship of icons, her council in the Temple of the Holy Apostles in Constantinople was broken up by troops. The following year the Seventh Ecumenical Council at Nicaea restored their use. However, for nearly a hundred years, the open warfare between the iconoclasts and the iconodules raged. As late as 815, Leo V stripped the churches of their sacramental ornaments and had their walls scraped and smeared with ashes. Ironically, while Christian images were destroyed, pagan images and those depicting earthly pleasure were preserved.

▲ **Interior of the church of St Catherine's monastery**

Icons were used as the focus of prayer in day-to-day religious worship

The conflict between the iconoclasts and the iconodules – after centuries of deadly opposition that had resulted in the loss of innumerable lives as well as icons – only came to an end when, in 842, the Emperor Theophilus died and his widow Theodora assumed the position of regent. Like many other Byzantine ladies before her – notably the Empress Irene – Theodora had kept icons hidden in her private rooms and had worshipped them in secret. On 11 March 843, Theodora issued an edict that gave permission for the worship of icons once more. This date is still celebrated as a holiday in the Orthodox Church.

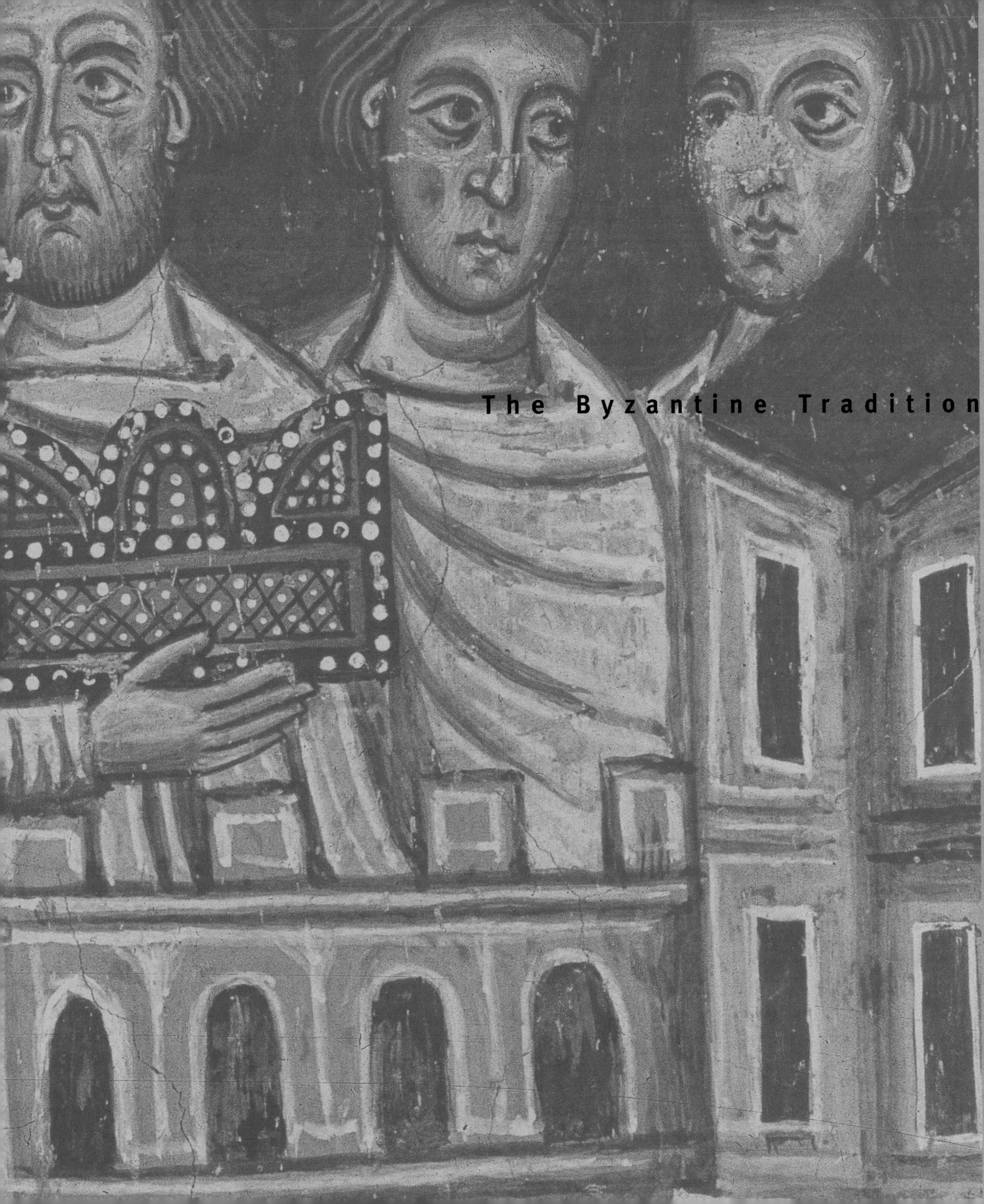

The Byzantine Tradition 2

On 11 May 330, the Emperor Constantine the Great established the new capital of the Roman Empire at the small port of Byzantium on the shores of the Bosphorus. In celebration a statue of Constantine Helios was carried in procession around the streets. It was, in fact, a bronze statue of Apollo, but its head had been replaced with a likeness of the emperor. Around it was a sunburst, with the sun's rays, it was said, made out of the nails that had fixed Christ to the cross. Within two hundred years, Byzantium – renamed Constantinople after Emperor Constantine – rivalled the wealth and power of Rome itself.

Sadly, because of the destruction wreaked by the iconoclasts, little is known of the early icons produced there. Only those preserved in St Catherine's monastery on Mount Sinai afford a clue. Two are of such quality that they have been ascribed to the studios of Constantinople and have been dated to the sixth or seventh century. This period is considered the first golden age of Byzantine art.

▶ **Emperor Constantine the Great**
The new capital of the Roman Empire was established by the emperor in 330 at the small port of Byzantium; two hundred years later it was renamed Constantinople in honour of its founder

One of the Sinai icons shows the Madonna and Child flanked by St George and St Theodore, the two great warrior saints of the early Christian church. They are dressed in the uniform of Imperial guards and are shown standing in the stiff frontal pose of earlier secular works. However, their skin tones – George is a pallid youth, Theodore is sun-tanned – are more realistic than their predecessors, especially when compared to the dark, olive-coloured shadows on the face of the Madonna. However, the Virgin's pose is much more fluid than the stances of the two saints who accompany her – her eyes are turned to the right and her knees to the left. Light streams down onto her head from the hand of God. In turn, two angels gaze up at it.

The faces of the angels are rendered in a third style. The paint is applied more thickly, the strokes are broader and they belong to a much older tradition, as if to convey that these creatures are not of this world. By contrast, the Christ child is painted in a realistic pose, his legs drawn up like a baby's. However, the head is that of an adult, with a high fore-head, stressing his divinity. This is the central focus of the icon. The use of competing styles indicates that the tradition of icon painting was only just crystallizing at the time this icon was produced.

The other early masterpiece found at the Sinai monastery is a half-figure of St Peter that is almost life-size. The depiction of his face – particularly of his hair and beard – is extremely lifelike for the period in which the icon was painted. Above him there are three medallions showing Christ flanked by the Virgin and a youthful St John the Evangelist. These portraits are rendered in the older, flatter style. All four figures have a penetrating gaze that directly engages the viewer.

The use of medallions in this way is rather reminiscent of the Egyptian paintings from Fayum. Medallions also commonly appeared in Imperial paintings of the period. However, the robes of St Peter are rendered in an almost impressionistic style, which, again, seems extraordinary for a paint-ing produced in the seventh century. This icon also displays the beginnings of the stylized ornamentation of highlights that later became common in Byzantine painting. Both icons employ the encaustic technique seen in Egyptian mummy portraits.

Although early icon painting borrows heavily from the artistic tech-niques and styles of the pre-Christian era, what was new was the subject

► **Madonna and Child flanked by St George and St Theodore**
This icon, discovered at St Catherine's monastery on Mount Sinai, is a rare example of the first golden age of Byzantine art (complete icon pictured on the right, details of the image are shown overleaf on pages 30 and 31)

matter – particularly scenes from the Bible. Another of the early Sinai icons, also painted using the encaustic technique, shows the three Hebrews in the Fiery Furnace. The three stand amid spirals of flame in Persian costume. An angel touches one of them on the shoulder. Even though this is a scene from the Old Testament, the angel holds a cross-shaped staff, signifying, perhaps, that in times to come they would be saved by the cross of Christ.

The style again is flat and thickset, with simplified outlines in the antique tradition. However, the highlights are highly ornamented and there are small circles of shiny white dots on the three Hebrews' cloaks. Other Sinai icons also displayed this particular technique of ornamentation, and it is thought to have originally developed in Jerusalem.

A long tunic worn by Christ in an icon depicting the crucifixion shows these same circles of dots, as does the cloak of the Virgin Mary, who is standing nearby. On the other side of the cross is John. This composition became standardized in later icons.

This is also the earliest icon to show Christ with his eyes closed and wearing a crown of thorns. This was the beginning of a tradition that was to extend right through the Middle Ages. Unusually, however, the two thieves crucified on either side of Christ have their Apocryphal names, Gestas and Dimas, written alongside them.

Stylistically speaking, this icon has parallels with the fresco depicting the crucifixion in the church of Santa Maria Antiqua in Rome, which dates from the middle of the eighth century. If the Sinai icon of the crucifixion also originates from the eighth century, it was executed at a time when the iconoclasts were in control and icons were banned from the empire. This therefore leads experts to believe that the icon was painted in Palestine. Since Palestine was under Muslim control at that time, the Imperial writ was of no significance there and icons could be produced without danger of persecution.

It was in the monastery of St Saba near Jerusalem around 730 that St John of Damascus wrote his *Discourses on Sacred Images,* in which he defended the use of icons. His work was essentially designed to encourage the continued production of icons in Palestine and many of the images preserved in the monastery of St Catherine on Mount Sinai were produced in Jerusalem during that period.

▶ **St Catherine's monastery, Mount Sinai**
Many early Byzantine icons were preserved by the monks of St Catherine's during periods of religious turmoil

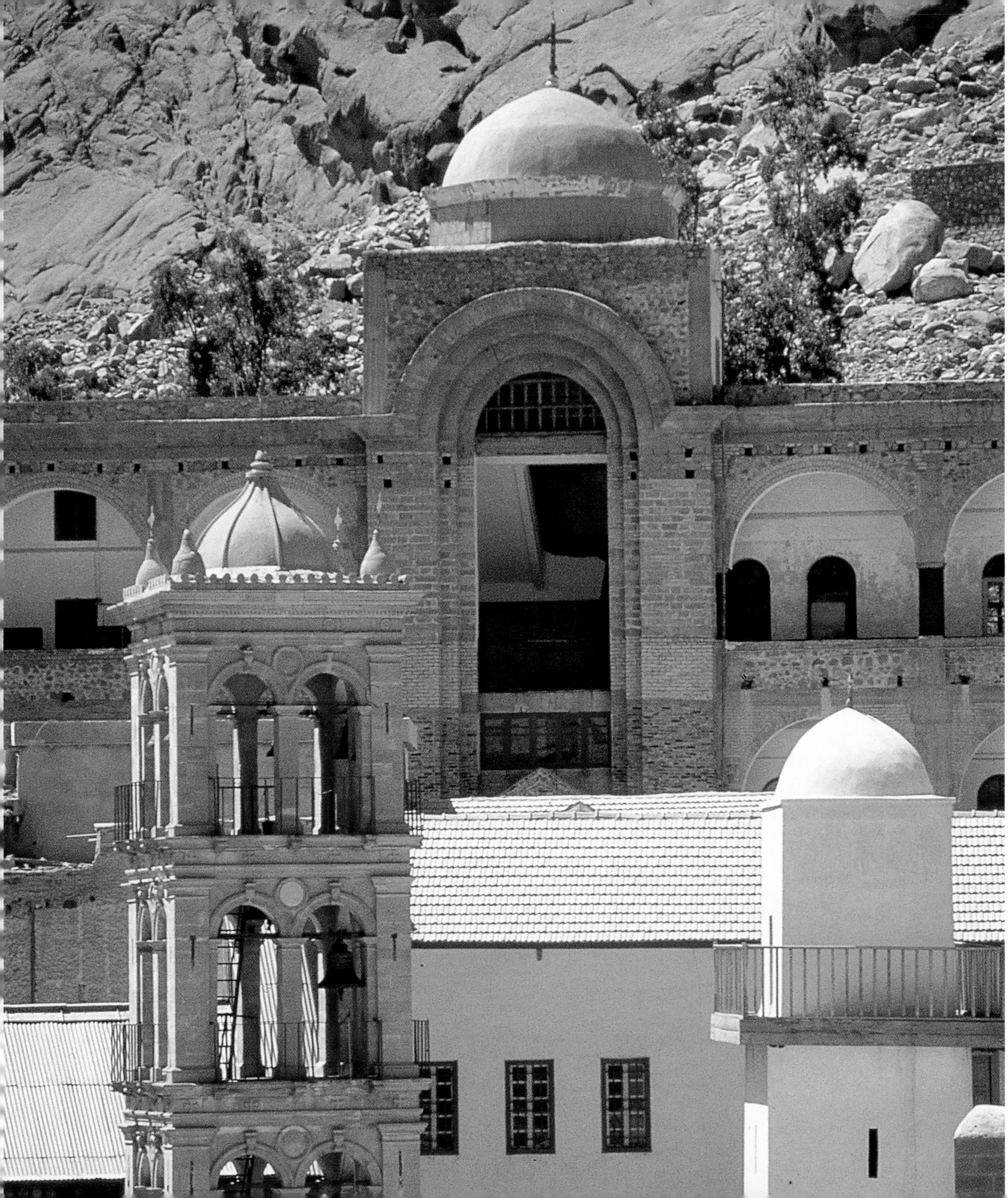

The Macedonian Renaissance 3

After Theodora's edict re-establishing the icon as an object of veneration, there began the second golden age of Byzantine art, also known as the Macedonian Renaissance. Icons from this period also found their way to Sinai. One showing the seated figure of the apostle Thaddeus illustrates the spirit of the Macedonian Renaissance. It employs the new light pastel colours that were coming into use in miniature painting and manuscript illumination at the time.

This icon of St Thaddeus is fluid and plastic, while other contemporary icons depict the saints, monks and fathers of the Church in a much more ethereal fashion as if they were detached from the world. However, all the icons of the period have a painterly quality borrowed from late antiquity or the early Christian era.

The painterly style hardens towards the end of the tenth century under the influence of the enamel work that was popular at the time. Icon painters try to emulate the brilliant surfaces of enamel in their work. In an icon of the young apostle Philip from this period, the impressionistic brushwork of the robes in earlier icons was dropped in favour of a hard, stylized rendition of the folds. Although this makes the figure appear as if it is sculpted in marble, experts believe that the artist did not borrow this style from the sculptures of antiquity, but rather from the ivory carving that was in vogue at that time.

Just as the style became more rigid, so did the conventions. The slightest deviation in the depiction of the beard or hair of a saint would lead the viewer to think that some other figure was intended.

By this time, the idea of a prototype – a concept first coined by St Basil in the fourth century – had become firmly established. By prototype, St Basil had meant a sacred personage, but the word soon came to mean the earliest icon of that person. The divine grace of a new icon was thought to be transmitted by how closely it resembled that first icon or prototype. So once the image of a saint had been established, that image would be endlessly repeated.

This was not just a convention. Although the artist was allowed some freedom of expression, detailed requirements for the depiction of the

▶ **First-century carved ivory figure**

A figurative example of fine ivory carving, which is thought to have influenced the early development of the depiction of the figure in icon painting

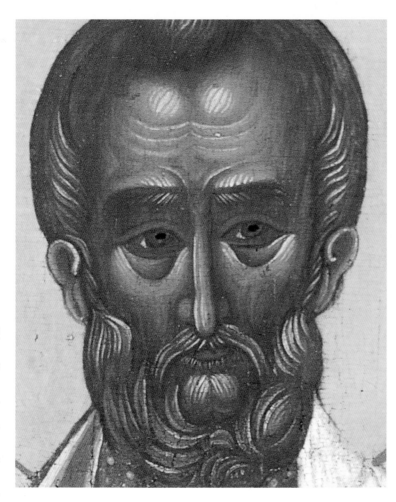

▲ ▶ St Nicholas

These three icons depict the saint according to his established 'prototype' image –
high forehead and carefully arranged hair and beard – in order that his identity was
immediately apparent to the viewer at a time when most people were illiterate

saints had been laid down by the Seventh (and last) Ecumenical Council at Nicaea in 787. The specifications were fixed from descriptions in the biographies of saints and laid out in a book called *The Herminia*, which all Byzantine icon painters followed. The idea was that there should be so little deviation in the depiction of the saints that the viewer should be able to recognize the icon without having to read the inscription. After all, few people at that time could read.

St Nicholas, a favourite subject of icons, is always shown with an overly high forehead and ornately primped and combed hair and beard. In one tenth-century icon of him, Nicholas is shown surrounded by miniatures of other saints. In the following century the use of a border of miniatures became more lavish. These are often rendered in cloisonné enamel, the saints depicted being ranked in a strict hierarchy.

During the course of the eleventh century, icons developed the precious feel of enamel. Golden halos were added and the leaf was treated with a circular roughing so that the halo appeared to rotate. The crucified Christ

begins to appear naked, draped only in a transparent loincloth. Previously he had been robed. The rendition of the body reveals a considerable understanding of anatomy, though Christ's body was often elongated to give it the appearance of an ethereal weightlessness.

It was in Constantinople particularly that a new technical perfection was achieved. Here, there was a great attention to detail that seems to have been borrowed from manuscript illumination. Icon painters in this city appear to have also worked as miniaturists and illuminators. This influence comes through, not just in the technique, but also in the narrative style of the icons they produced.

The miniatures added around the frame of the icon came to depict scenes from the lives of the saints. Triptychs became popular, too, and a story was told in a number of scenes across the panels. One triptych panel of the period has as its central image the Virgin of the Annunciation. Alongside there are two scenes from the life of St Nicholas – one showing him being ordained as a priest, the second showing him being anointed as a bishop. Sadly, the rest of the triptych is missing and it would have shown six scenes from the life of St Nicholas in all.

Another eleventh-century icon illustrates the Nativity and Infancy of Christ. Individual episodes have the appearance of miniature theatrical tableaux distributed over a mountain range. The icon's central image, the Nativity itself, is set inside a cave, and is framed by scenes showing the angel announcing Christ's birth to the shepherds and the arrival, adoration and departure of the Magi. Running down the icon are scenes of Joseph's dream and the Flight into Egypt, the Massacre of the Innocents and Elizabeth's Concealment of the Infant John. All these scenes are common in illustrated manuscripts of the time. One scene – showing midwives bringing water to bathe the new-born child – is unique, though it, too, is thought to have been copied from an illuminated manuscript now lost.

Another icon of the eleventh or twelfth century whose origin is assumed to be a manuscript shows the ladder to heaven. There are thirty rungs on the ladder, corresponding to the virtues expounded by John Climacus, who

◄ ► Greek icon showing Christ on the cross

Icons began to depict Christ naked on the cross at this time, dressed only in a loincloth (complete icon pictured opposite, detail shown on the left)

was the abbot of the monastery on Mount Sinai. Climacus's treatise, which has 30 chapters, appears as a great number of manuscripts and such an illustration would have made a fitting frontispiece. In the icon, some of the monks making the ascent are dragged from the ladder by demons representing the vices. The only monk to make it to the top is John Climacus himself. He is followed one rung down by Archbishop Anthony, who is thought to have succeeded Climacus as abbot of the monastery.

In the twelfth century a new type of icon emerged. It showed the twelve great feasts of the Christian calendar or the lives of the saints, and was designed to run in sequence along a beam at the top of the iconostasis, above the architrave. Sometimes the sequence was interrupted by a central Deëis, which was either another image of the Virgin or else a repetition of the central theme of the iconostasis.

The style of these icons gradually became more solid in form and more monumental. There was a change in the use of colour, too. Instead of luminous pastels, more saturated colours were used that gave off a warm glow and deepened the drama of the scene being depicted. Also, for the first time, emotions were expressed in icons. This was because icon painters began to draw their influence from frescos in the same way that they had drawn inspiration from miniatures the century before. Particularly influential were the frescos at Nerezi, painted in 1164, which show the Lamentation over the Dead Christ.

◄ **Twelfth-century fresco of Christ being taken from the cross**
The emotional content of Biblical scenes inspired fresco painters' visions of Christ's life, and these in turn influenced icon artists to draw on the expressive potential of the subjects they depicted

▶ **The ladder to heaven**
Eleventh- or twelfth-century Byzantine icon depicting the monks of Sinai attempting to climb the ladder to heaven, all failing except the abbot, John Climacus

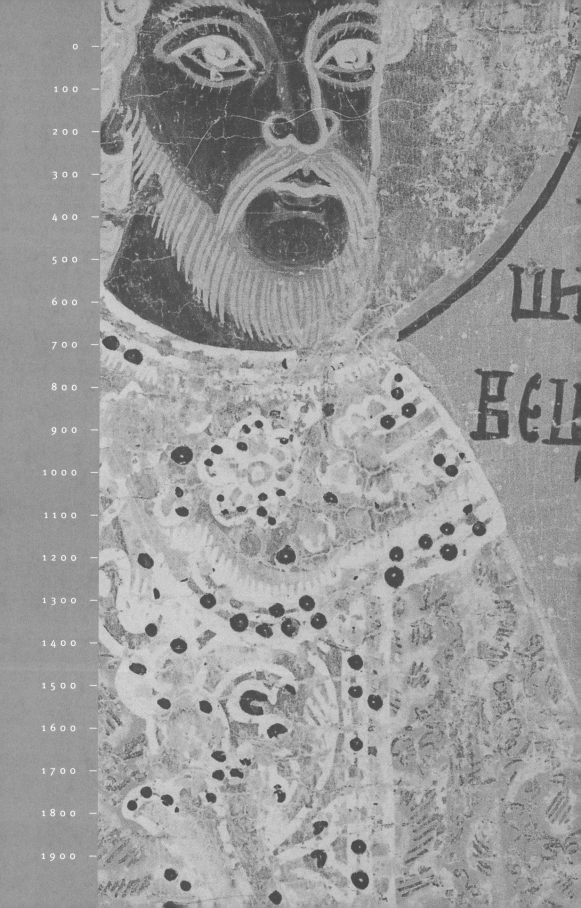

Icons Spread Westwards

4

Until the end of the twelfth century, the finest icons are assumed to have come from Constantinople. However, Byzantine techniques had been widely copied in Italy and began spreading from there across the Balkans. By the time Constantinople fell in 1453, an important centre of icon production already existed at Salonica. Icons were also produced on Mount Athos, though many of the examples found there were imported to the area from a number of other places. A distinctive style of icon painting developed in Cyprus.

Crete is well known for its murals of the fourteenth and fifteenth centuries, but little is known of its icon output during that period. Some icons from the sixteenth and seventeenth centuries have been traced back to Crete, or to Cretan artists working abroad. Icons are, of course, easily transportable. Many are even specifically designed to be transported: they were painted on both sides – though, of course, only one side could be seen when they hung on the iconostasis – because they were paraded through the streets.

In the twelfth century icons were still rare in Greece. Those that have survived were largely found in discarded corners of the monasteries on Mount Athos. The icon discovered there dates from the twelfth century. It is a small icon of St Panteleimon and was discovered in the monastery of Lavra. It has the almond eyes and the fine features of the famous Virgin of Vladimir, now in Moscow. The use of rosy flesh and greenish shadows is common to both works.

An early icon of St Peter, also found in the monasteries of Mount Athos, shows the apostle with an open manuscript. This is reminiscent of portraits of the philosophers from the pre-Christian era and was a staple of murals of the time.

The move towards monumentality continued, especially in icons depicting the twelve great feast days of the Christian year. One icon from Greece depicting the Raising of Lazarus has been shown to be by the same artist who painted the icon of the Transfiguration that is now in St Petersburg. The brown flesh tones, white strokes on the highlights and red brush-strokes on the cheeks and foreheads lead experts to believe that both icons are from the same series.

Carved and painted wooden architrave beams began to appear in iconostases in Mount Athos in the twelfth century. Although mural

► **Nativity of Christ**
Fifteenth-century icon by a Cretan artist, employing the traditional Byzantine techniques that had by this time spread across the Balkans to Greece

painting was very much in vogue at that time, icon paintings continued to retain some of the qualities of the miniaturist, making the artists' work separate and distinct.

However, one style is borrowed directly from monumental artists: the use of mosaics. Mosaic icons were made in the eleventh and twelfth centuries, using exactly the same techniques as wall mosaics but scaled down to icon size. Interestingly, there had been an early encaustic mosaic icon style. Instead of painting the hot wax and pigment onto the icon with a brush, tiny cubes were applied, building up the image in the same way as a conventional mosaic.

One double-sided icon from Epius, now in the Byzantine Museum in Athens, is of particular interest. It has long puzzled experts because it shows no artistic unity at all. One side of the icon depicts the traditional image of Christ on the cross, flanked by the Virgin Mary and St John. However, when it was restored, it was shown to have had contributions from three distinct periods, stretching from the ninth century to the thirteenth. The Virgin and Child on the other side of the icon was from the sixteenth century.

A similar double-sided icon from Cyprus reveals Western influences. This is doubtless due to the fact that, from 1192, Cyprus was under the occupation of French crusaders, who went on to take Constantinople in 1203, sacking it in 1204 and occupying it until 1261.

Other Western elements crept into Byzantine icons. Another double-sided icon from the Byzantine Museum in Athens shows the life and martyrdom of St George. The soldier saint carries a shield divided into four fields, like those of the crusaders, though the inscription around the outside is in a pseudo-Cufic script, indicating that its origins lie further to the east. The icon also has carved relief. There are records of early Byzantine carved stone icons and precious icons, such as those made in gold and enamel in the Cathedral Treasury in St Mark's, Venice, but carved wooden icons are rare.

At the end of the thirteenth century, mosaic icons shrank until the stones used were the size of a grain of sand. They were covered with precious metal, inset with enamel. By the beginning of the fourteenth century, artists were packing them with figures. A single icon might show the entire twelve feasts of the Christian calendar.

◄ **Panel from the golden altar of St Mark's Cathedral, Venice**
This stunning tenth-century altar panel is made with gold, silver, enamel, precious stones and pearls (the whole altar is shown overleaf on pages 50 and 51)

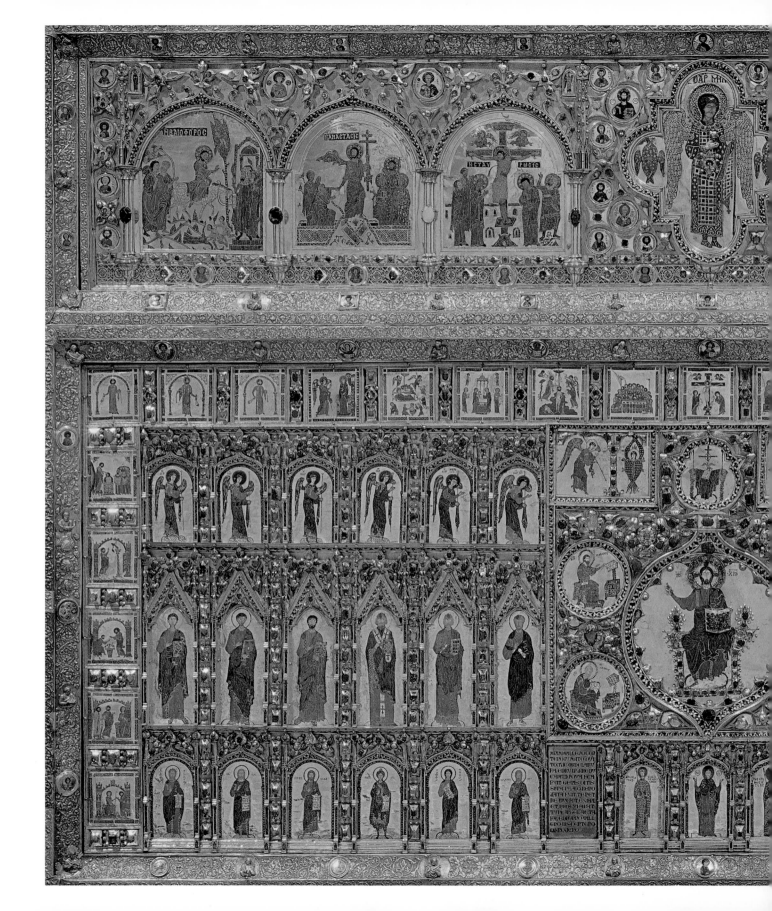

Icons Spread Westwards

Compassion became a significant element in icons of the fourteenth century – with either the Virgin Mary providing it or Christ on the cross inviting it. Eastern artists also felt free to incorporate Western influences, such as heraldic devices and a realistic portrayal of the human form. However, faces and figures were still painted only directly from the front, in a manner borrowed from classical antiquity. Light and shade were used to model form, though this sometimes degenerated into simple strokes of white paint on projecting areas. The central theme of these works seems to be the portrayal of beauty. Although beauty is a classical ideal, it was thought that Christ, the Virgin Mary and other sacred figures had attained it through virtue and suffering.

Architrave painting spread throughout Greece. In the centre, a Great Deësis would be composed of up to fifteen half-length icons showing Christ sitting in Judgment, flanked by the Virgin Mary, St John, the apostles and other saints. These icons came from Constantinople and spread across the Balkans, some even finding their way to Russia.

The painting of sacred figures in icons and the conventions of ordinary portraiture began to overlap. In the icon of the Incredulity of Thomas from the monastery of Meteora, sacred figures mingle with real people – this was an extraordinary, even revolutionary, idea at that time. Christ is shown touching a woman and the head of a man who is not one of the apostles. The man has been identified as Thomas Preljubovic, Lord of Jannina (1361–84). It is hardly a flattering portrait, but then Preljubovic had an unpleasant reputation as a Serb despot. The woman is his wife, the Serb princess, Maria Palaeologina. She has been identified from other portraits and the artist seems to have rendered a true likeness. This broke the rigid conventions of the icon and, even though the real figures stand out from the formulaic rendition of the apostles, the apostles too are presented in quarter profile – again, a new departure.

The breaking of the old, rigid conventions gave icons a new dynamism in the second half of the fourteenth century. The subject matter of the icons involved the depiction of suffering, grief and pain. St John joined the Virgin Mary on the same side of the cross in order to comfort her, as in the Crucifixion icon from the Chapel of the Annunciation on the island of Patmos. This leaves room for the sponge bearer, the centurion and a crowd of spectators who, along with the central figure of Christ, form a

► **The Mother of God**

By the end of the thirteenth century, icon painters were attempting to convey the full emotional intensity and passion of the scenes they portrayed (complete icon pictured on the right, detail on page 55)

overleaf ► **The Mother of God**
Thirteenth-century Serbian icon

triangular composition. A second triangle is formed at Christ's feet by three people dividing his clothes.

Another icon depicting the Crucifixion and following the same prototype formed the lid of the reliquary presented to Venice's Scuola della Carità by the Greek Cardinal, Bessarion, in 1463. It shows the Virgin Mary with a group of holy women on one side of the cross, while St John – more conventionally – is on the other side along with the sponge bearer, the centurion and the onlookers. Again, three people at Christ's feet can be seen dividing his clothes.

In both of these icons the key figures are rendered elongated, slim and weightless. This tendency to idealize the figures in icon painting reaches its zenith with the Hospitality of Abraham in the Benaki Museum, Athens, and the Archangel Michael in the Civic Museum of Pisa. This latter may be an icon of Italian origin.

By the fifteenth century, the influence of Italian art appears regularly in Greek icons. In the icon of the Dormition of the Virgin from the monastery of St John on Patmos there are buildings with peaked roofs and rose

► **The evangelist Matthew**
Late thirteenth-century Serbo-Byzantine icon

►► **Archangel Gabriel**
Fourteenth-century Greco-Serbian fresco in the Church of Christ's Ascension, Decani

► **The Virgin Mary**
Detail of a fourteenth-century Serbo-Byzantine icon

windows that come straight out of Giotto. They are also rendered in perspective, another Italian innovation.

Another rose window appears in an illustration of the Magnificat in the Byzantine Museum in Athens. This icon is unusual in that it teems with a multitude of tiny figures. Byzantine in flavour, the icon may have been painted in Crete, where chapels of that era often incorporated Western-style rose windows.

Some of the great icon painters of Constantinople had already moved to Crete before the city's fall in 1453. By the sixteenth century Crete was the semi-official home of painting for the Orthodox Church. Many of its artists struggled to hold on to the Byzantine traditions of the fourteenth and fifteenth centuries. Local artists, such as Michael Damaskinos, even adopted early Byzantine traditions in their icons – though Damaskinos defied convention by signing his name on his Descent into Limbo, which is now in the Benaki Museum in Athens. Until then icon painters had not signed their work. After all, icons were supposed to be produced by God, not by the hand of man.

Other icon artists soon followed suit, however. In the seventeenth century, Emmanuel Tzane both signed and dated his 1637 icon of St Anne with

the Virgin Mary holding a flower, which is also in the Benaki Museum in Athens. Even among those icon painters who maintained the traditional anonymity, few could resist the use of perspective, chiaroscuro and pastoral motifs that were borrowed from the Italian school.

Icons may have reached the central Balkans as early as AD 400. Although none has survived, fresco paintings in a tomb in ancient Sofia show portraits of the archangels in the iconic style of early Greek work. Other frescos and mosaics in iconic style from the seventh century are found in the 'Red Church' near Perustice in the Plovidic area.

The first Bulgarian kingdom was established in 681, but it was largely non-Christian. Christianity became the state religion only in 865. After that, icons were brought back by pilgrims who had visited Jerusalem. The iconoclast controversy, however, had significantly less effect in the Balkans than it had elsewhere. John Exarchos, whose life straddled the turn of the tenth century, translated St John of Damascus's *Discourses on Sacred Images*, defending the use of icons, into his native tongue.

Another eloquent defence of icons was written by Presbyter Cosmas. He talked of kissing the icon of the Virgin Mary and kneeling before images of God – though he pointed out, along the lines of the Council of Nicaea, that he was not praying to the paint or the wood, but rather to the figure portrayed there. He said that when he prayed to the icon of a saint, he was asking the saint to pray for him.

Many of the icons in the early Bulgarian capital, Preslav, came from Constantinople, but local icon painters produced work of the same high standard. In fact, one icon of the Virgin was carried back to Constantinople as a trophy of war by Emperor Jon Tsimiskes after he had sacked the Bulgarian capital in 972.

Sadly, only one of the Preslav icons has survived. It was painted on clay plaques instead of wood and was found in fragments in the ruins of the monastery of Patlejna, near Preslav. It shows a life-size portrait of St Theodore. Other fragments of clay icons have been found. They follow the same prototypes as Byzantine wooden and enamel icons, although they carry Slavic inscriptions.

The first golden age of Bulgarian art ended when the Byzantines invaded the country in 1018. During the occupation icons were still produced, but none has survived. When the Bulgarians revolted in 1185, the Byzantines

► **Cardinal Bessarion worshipping in front of a reliquary of the cross**
This image of the Greek cardinal, from the door of a church tabernacle, shows the devotional use of icons in fifteenth-century worship

found an icon of St Demetrius taken from Salonica in a fortress near the capital Tirnovo. Its recapture was the cause of great rejoicing and the Byzantine Emperor Isaac II Angelus ordered that a cover of precious metals be made for it.

However, the revolt succeeded and there was a new flourishing of artistic endeavour in the Balkans, especially in the production of frescos and icons. Although none of the icons survived, frescos frequently carried pseudo-icons – framed areas depicting iconographic themes. These are assumed to be copies of icons.

There were certainly icons being painted in Bulgaria at the time. One, which became known as La Sainte Face de Laon, was taken to Rome and then, in 1249, on to the Cathedral of Laon in northern France. It showed a mandylion, the face of Christ impressed on a linen cloth, which had been a popular subject of icons since the creation of the famous mandylion of Edessa, reputed to have cured King Abgar of Edessa of leprosy and to have given the Imperial Roman army victory at Edessa in Turkey in 544. Mandylions had been widely spread throughout Christendom during the ninth and tenth centuries.

Bulgarian icons were also distributed throughout the Balkans and some found their way to Russia. However, it is often difficult to discover the provenance of an icon, since copies traditionally carried the name of the church or monastery where the original was found, rather than the name of the place where it was painted.

Among the most outstanding works of the late fourteenth century, now in the Archaeological Museum in Sofia, is the doubled-sided icon presented to the Monastery of St John the Evangelist near Poganovo by Helena, wife of the Byzantine Emperor Manuel II Palaeologus, who was also the granddaughter of Tsar Ivan Alexander. Her father, the local Prince Constantine Dejanov, had founded the monastery and Helena presented the costly icon to the monks in 1395 after her father fell in battle at Wallachia, fighting the Turks.

One side of the icon shows the Virgin Mary with St John the Evangelist, patron of the monastery, and is rendered in the elongated Byzantine style. On the other side of the icon is a copy of the *Miracle in the Monastery of Christ Latom*, a mosaic found in the apse of the Church of Christ Latom in Salonica.

▶ **Medieval fresco depicting Christ**
This ceiling painting is from the Cathedral of St Sofia in Macedonia

СТЫ НІКОЛАЕ ИЗБАВИ Ѿ РОКА Ѿ ПЛЕНА

This icon is one of the few works of art to survive from this period, since Bulgaria fell to the Turks in 1396 and, until 1878, it was part of the Ottoman Empire. Churches were looted and burned. Some were converted to mosques, and priests and monks destroyed icons and other sacred objects to save them from sacrilege. Even those icons that were hidden were clumsily restored.

It was not until the seventeenth century that the Ottomans allowed the Bulgarians to build new churches, which were quickly decorated with frescos and icons. According to the historian Pajsije, who wrote the *Slavic Bulgarian History* in 1762, there was a particularly talented icon painter living in Bulgaria in the first half of the seventeenth century. He was a monk named Pimen, who had learned his craft on Mount Athos. He was not the only one to come from Athos, but there were also centres of indigenous craftsmanship at Sofia, Vraca, Tirnovo, Nessebri and the monastery of Etropole.

While earlier icon painters remained anonymous, these men signed their names – Yerey Gergin, Nedelko the Painter, Vassili the Monk, Stamen the Painter and a priest named Peter, Lord of Toma. They were followed in the eighteenth century by Nicholas, two teachers named Tson and Kosta respectively, Panaiot the Painter and Thomas Vishanov. They signed their names in Greek since that was the official language of the Church.

These artists remained largely faithful to the old traditions. Their guide to their art was a hand-written copy of the Byzantine *Herminia*, called *The Erminiji*. Unlike the Byzantines, these artists generally painted on a gold background, using ethereal poses and bright colours. Silver and gilt cases that covered everything but the faces of the figures in the icon were also used. The cases were decorated with floral motifs, religious emblems and portraits of the saints in low relief. However, Bulgarian icon painters were as unable to resist Western influences as their Byzantine counterparts. Baroque and Rococo motifs, and then Western styles of composition, quickly began to appear in their work. However, the Bulgarians did not adopt the use of perspective.

St George and St Demetrius, both portrayed on horseback, were popular themes, along with local Bulgarian saints. In addition, portraits of the people who commissioned the icons crept in. Frescos and other murals were also used as sources.

◄ **Sacred images of saints**
In the eighteenth and nineteenth centuries, Bulgarian artists began to produce simplified copies of the popular saints that had once only been available to those with the money to commission unique works of art (the saint illustrated on the left is St Nicholas)

overleaf ► **St George**
A seventeenth-century icon of St George slaying the dragon is shown on page 64

overleaf ► **St Demetrius**
An early eighteenth-century Serbian icon of St Demetrius is shown on page 65

Icons Spread Westwards

No Bulgarian mosaic icons have been discovered, though mosaic murals have survived. Two rare relief icons from the turn of the thirteenth century, showing the apostles Peter and Paul, were found in the excavation of a church at the fortress of Tsepena.

In the eighteenth and nineteenth centuries, the demand for icons was so great that cheap copies were made by folk artists. These primitive works maintained the same iconography and prototypes, but their freer style is more expressive. They incorporated ordinary people and scenes of everyday life into their icons.

Icons also began to appear everywhere – in private homes as well as in churches. In homes they were hung on an east wall or in a corner. Diptychs and triptychs were commonly used to make a small private chapel in the home and they were venerated.

In churches, iconostases became larger, extending to two or three storeys, with numerous tiers of icons. This made the tradition of kissing icons difficult and smaller portable icons were introduced that were set on a special pedestal, or proskynitarion, during festivals.

Icons spread from the iconostasis along the entrance walls of churches, too. Here, they often illustrated Biblical stories. In Bulgaria there was also a unique tradition of didactic icons, showing how to take communion, make confession or live a more virtuous life.

Early Serbian icons were painted by Greeks – and were valued all the more because of that fact. However, local artists also began painting icons. These icons appeared in cases of beaten silver and many were believed to be capable of performing miracles. Unfortunately, they were destroyed during the twelfth century under the instructions of the Bogomils, a heretical sect. However, iconic images were preserved in frescos painted on church walls.

The earliest icon from a Serbian monastery is a Virgin and Child in a Bulgarian style, dating from the late twelfth century. It is a mosaic icon, using large stones like a wall mosaic. It survived in the monastery of Chilander on Mount Athos.

In the early thirteenth century, Serbia became a kingdom. St Sava set up an independent Church, expelling the Greek bishops. He re-established the cult of the icon, founded a monastery on Mount Athos and brought in icon painters from Constantinople.

◄ **St Luke painting the Virgin, by Cretan artist Michael Damaskinos**
The painting of icons was believed to be a sacred act in itself. The aim of the painter was to recreate the the image of the earliest 'prototype' of his subject, which would ensure that divine grace would be passed on from icon to icon

St Sava and his brother, Stefan Nemanja, the first king of an autonomous Serbia, were among the many wealthy donors who gave a large number of icons to the newly liberated country's monasteries. Some of these were produced locally, though St Sava commissioned at least two from Salonica. Several icons were decorated with gold wreaths, pearls and precious gems.

The tomb of Stefan Nemanja at Studenica is decorated with frescos that incorporate two imitation icons. The bright colours and the simplified style, as well as the distinctly Slavic look of the Madonna, mark a considerable deviation from their Byzantine prototypes.

In 1281, Queen Beloslava, the wife of King Vladislav, deposited an inventory of the family's icon collection in the Dubrovnik archives. Along with the standard religious items is a family portrait, a silver-cased icon of St Simeon Nemanja, founder of the dynasty. Two miniatures that were naïve copies of icons were destroyed in a fire during the bombardment of Belgrade in 1941.

The renaissance of Byzantine art that followed the expulsion of the crusaders from Constantinople in 1262 spread across the Balkans and, as a result, icon painters achieved sufficient fame to become known by their first names. An icon of St George from Struga, dated 1266–7, bears an inscription on the back that identifies the donor as John the Deacon, and the artist as another man named John, who describes himself as an 'official historian'. Eutychios and Michael were two particularly well-known icon painters in Ohrid.

Shortly before 1300, a large icon of St Matthew the Evangelist was painted in Ohrid. It borrowed its style directly from the classical Byzantine work of the tenth century. Romanesque influences came from the south-west and directly across the Adriatic from Apulia in Italy. It was a two-way traffic: icons made in the workshops at Kotor, the Serbian port on the Adriatic, found their way to Rome.

Icon painting was considered the highest form of art during this period. Although its exponents had once borrowed from mural art, icon painting now dominated fresco work. Earlier full-length icons now gave way to half-length figures.

In the fourteenth century iconostases filled up with miniature icons. The older, larger icons were fixed in place and were removed only in the event

▶ **John the Baptist**
Thirteenth-century icon discovered at the Serbian
monastery of Chilandar on Mount Athos

of an earthquake or a fire. The smaller icons were taken outdoors for feast days and carried through the streets. Again, they were painted on both sides for the purposes of such celebratory parades, though not necessarily by the same artist.

Icon painting survived the victory of the Turks over the Serbs at Smederevo in 1459. Indeed, it flourished. The iconostases were soon full up and Serbian monks, under Western influence, erected smaller iconostases with altars, in addition to the principal one. Travellers who stayed at the monasteries in the Balkans in the sixteenth century were amazed by the huge number of icons. In churches they spread to the choir as well as standing on special tables or proskynitaria.

At the beginning of the sixteenth century, the Serb state collapsed and the nobility were dispersed. Greek and Italian styles took over, but in remote areas Serbian icon painters consciously opposed Western influences, borrowing ornamental elements from the Eastern and Russian traditions. During the late sixteenth and seventeenth centuries, Serbian icons became much prized in Russia.

The interest was such that a Russian translation of a *Herminia*, or icon painter's manual, was completed in 1599. It purported to be by a Serbian bishop, though it was more likely the work of an itinerant Greek painter who knew Serbian. Numerous similar manuals were published in Serbia.

In the early seventeenth century, a painter named George Mitrofanovic took Serbian icon and fresco painting to new heights at the monastery of Chilandar on Mount Athos. His two students, Cosmas and John, began incorporating Western ideas in order to give a fresh depth of psychological understanding to their portraiture. They were followed by a new generation of icon painters – the Chilandar priest, Danilo, who was a cold but brilliant technician; the prolific artist Radul, who inspired numerous followers; and the monk Avesalom Vujicic from the monastery of St Luke at Moraca. St Luke is the patron saint of painters.

While the Russians were seeking a way ahead in icon painting, the Serbs – located at the westernmost frontier of the Orthodox nations – stoutly defended the old traditions. However, in the late seventeenth century, the Turks were once again on the offensive and Serb icon painters quickly fled from their home country to Srem, Slavonia and Hungary. There they were engulfed by the Baroque.

▶ **Archangel Gabriel**
Fourteenth-century icon found at the monastery of Chilandar on Mount Athos

Kiev to Moscow – The Russian Schools

5

Russia was Christianized in the late tenth century under Prince Vladimir of Kiev. The city of Kiev, though now in the Ukraine, was the first capital of Russia. Vladimir had begun his reign in 980 with an orgy of paganism. He had taken numerous wives and had sacrificed thousands of his people to pagan gods. However, he then decided that religion would be good for his subjects, so he sent scouts to neighbouring lands to find one.

He was drawn to Islam because it promised the continuation of carnal pleasures after death, but its ban on alcohol discouraged him. It was impossible to live happily in Russia without strong drink, he said. He rejected the Church of Rome because he feared subjugation by the pope. However, he was attracted to Orthodoxy when he heard of the splendour of its celebration of the Eucharist and the beauty of its churches, particularly the Hagia Sophia Cathedral in Constantinople.

In 988, Vladimir was baptized into the Orthodox faith. This was followed by the enforced baptism of all his subjects in the Dnieper River in 989. Over the next thirty years, four hundred churches were built in Kiev alone. Artists were brought from Constantinople to decorate them and to teach local artists how to make the icons required for Orthodox worship.

In 1036, Kiev's own Hagia Sophia was founded and in 1051 the first monastery on Russian soil, the Monastery of the Caves, was built by St Anthony, spiritual leader of the Russian monastery on Mount Athos. The first Russian icon painters, Alimpii and Grigorii, were trained at the Monastery of the Caves. None of their work survived, but murals showing Vladimir's grandchildren still grace the walls of the monastery.

The earliest surviving icons painted in Russia are so Byzantine in style that they cannot be regarded as truly Russian. However, by the twelfth century, local schools were developing their own style, distinguished by its clear, bright colouring.

▶ **Hagia Sophia Cathedral, Constantinople**
The tenth-century ruler Prince Vladimir was impressed by the magnificence of Constantinople's churches. This contributed to his decision to introduce Christian Orthodoxy to Russia

overleaf ▶ **Monastery of the Caves**
Constructed in 1051, this was the first monastery to be built on Russian soil

following page ▶ **The Battle of Kozelsk**
In 1237 the Mongols invaded Russia

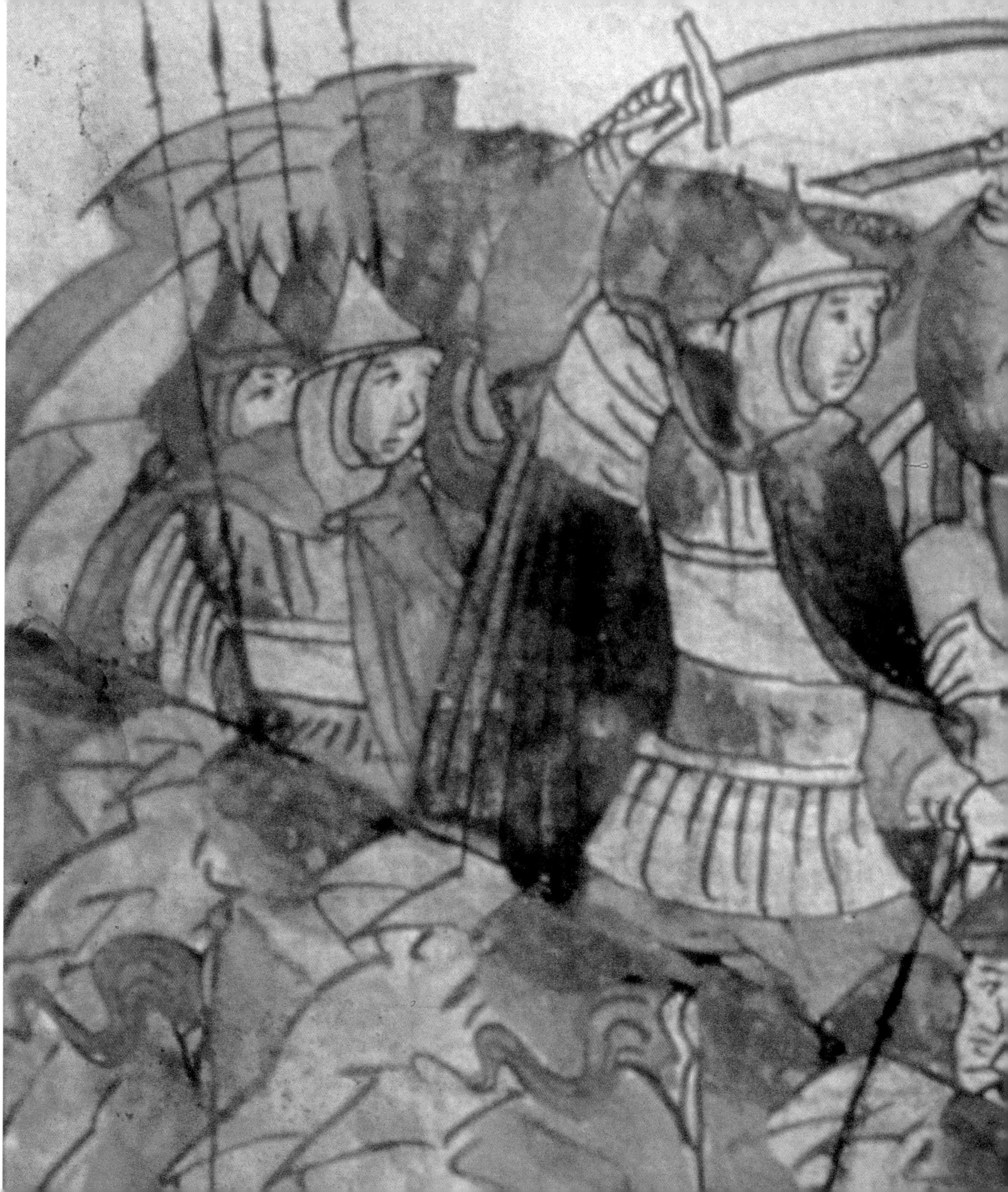

Kiev to Moscow – The Russian Schools

In 1157, Prince Andrew Bogolyubsky moved the Russian capital to Vladimir and Kiev lost its pre-eminence. Vladimir and its twin city of Suzdal became the centre of art. The influence of the Greeks was strong in the Vladimir-Suzdal School. The Byzantine use of impressionist techniques and modelling was retained, but the emotional character of Russian art began to show itself in the increasingly conscious use of expressive colour. Vladimir-Suzdal iconography also developed a standard set of facial expressions to convey specific emotions. Small hands were another characteristic peculiar to the Vladimir-Suzdal School.

Russia's links with Europe were weakened by the sack of Constantinople by the crusaders in 1204. Then in 1237 the Mongols invaded. The Vladimir-Suzdal School and what was left of the Kievian tradition were quickly swept away. Only Pskov and Novgorod escaped. There, icon painters worked unhindered.

Pskov had been a centre of fresco painting since the twelfth century. In 1156, the decoration of the Mirozhsk monastery was executed by Greek and local artists. Although their murals were still essentially standard Byzantine works, they already displayed the dark, brooding mood that characterizes Russian art. The Pskov icon style developed from the monumental style of its murals, using intense colour and strong, rhythmic composition. To start with, the Pskov icons outshone the more conservative work coming out of Novgorod.

Icons soon took over from fresco work as the major decoration in churches. In Pskov, once free from Greek influence, icon painters incorporated local peasant types and decorative motifs borrowed from folk art. Fiery reds and a deep 'Pskovian' olive green became closely associated with local artists. Their work was particularly well suited to the dark interiors of the churches in the northern city.

Nevertheless, it was Novgorod that became the cultural centre of Russia during the Mongol occupation. The city soon developed its own local style, which was more concerned with abstract patterns than the presence of the leading figures. It favoured lighter, brighter colours and softening of facial types. Modelled Byzantine form gave way to a greater use of line. This flattened figures and replaced the penetrating gaze of Byzantine icons with a dreamy, introspective look. However, it was the lyricism of the pattern and detail that carried that same emotional intensity seen in all Russian art.

▶ **The entombment of Christ**
During the occupation of Russia by the Mongols, the iconoclastic tradition survived and flourished in Novgorod

overleaf ▶ **The Mother of God**
The common subject of the madonna and child depicted by the icon painters of Pskov and Novgorod displays the similarities and differences of artistic interpretation that developed across Russia

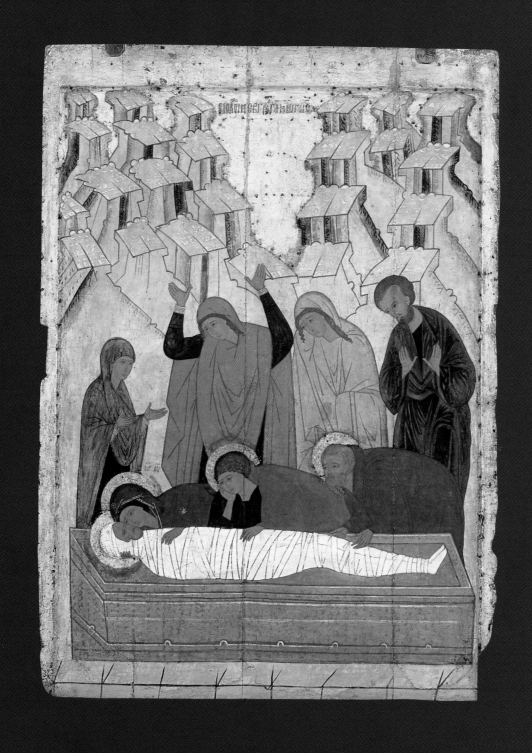

However, this artistic development slowed in the late thirteenth century as the Mongol threat grew. In the early fourteenth century, the city began to feel safer. It was then that the iconostasis was introduced into the Russian churches. Large numbers of icons were required to fill them and an explosion in production followed.

The introduction of iconostasis brought a new element to the icon. Each had to be a complete work of art in its own right but, in complex arrangements on the iconostasis, they all had to work together as a coherent whole. Russian icon painters achieved this with the use of strong lines and skilful colour harmonies. The silhouette became all-important and led to the elongation of the figure that is standard in Russian art.

The Byzantine influence continued. In the second half of the fourteenth century, a number of Greek artists arrived from Constantinople, bringing with them new subject matter. One of them was Theophanes the Greek (c. 1340–c. 1410), who was born in Constantinople and came to Novgorod in the 1370s to paint murals. However, he also received numerous commissions to paint icons and his work covers the complete range of icon painting. He merged a knowledge of late Byzantine monumental painting with the style of late Russian icon painting and his work has become the template for icon painters ever since.

Meanwhile, in the obscure town of Moscow, cut off from Byzantine influences, a new style of painting emerged. Its leading exponent was the native son, Andrei Rublev (c. 1360–1430). He had been a monk at the Trinity monastery in Zagorsk, where he received his artistic training.

Theophanes moved to Moscow when it was annexed by Novgorod and, in 1392, painted the icon of the Mother of God of the Don. It commemorated the Battle of Kulikovo where the Mongols were routed. Theophanes brought with him to Moscow a subtle appreciation of colour and an almost impressionistic manner of producing superbly expressive figures, but his greatest legacy to Muscovite painting was the use of curving planes.

In 1395, Theophanes supervised the internal decoration of the Kremlin's Church of the Nativity of the Virgin and, in 1405, began work on the Cathedral of the Annunciation. His assistant was Rublev. Even though they worked on iconostases together, Rublev's achievement owes almost nothing to the influence of Theophanes. However, the two of them are equally matched in artistic excellence.

▲ ▶ Transfiguration of Christ

Born and trained in Constantinople, Theophanes the Greek was to bring together the artistic heritage of his native city with the evolving styles of Russian icon painting to create the language of imagery that icon painters have adopted to this day
(complete icon pictured opposite, detail shown above and on page 88)

Rublev concentrated on luminous colour and delicacy of line. He eliminated superfluous detail and built up complex compositions with the remaining elements. Rublev alone directed the decoration of the Cathedral of the Assumption at Vladimir. His most famous icon, the Old Testament Trinity, was painted for the stone Cathedral of the Trinity at the monastery at Zagorsk, built in 1422 to replace the wooden one there. It is remarkably well preserved and its fresh use of colour and precisely worked-out composition was used as a model for icon painters until well into the nineteenth century.

When Rublev died in 1430, he was buried in Moscow in the monastery of Saviour-Andronikov. Under his influence and helped by renewed contact with Byzantium following the stemming of the Mongol tide, the Muscovite School flourished. By the beginning of the fifteenth century, it outshone all others. Its ascendancy was complete when, in 1510, Pskov was annexed by Moscow and, in 1547, a fire in Novgorod forced its artists to move to Moscow.

The city itself became pre-eminent when the Grand Dukes of Moscow finally drove out the Mongols and united the cities of central Russia. With the fall of Constantinople in 1453, Moscow became the centre of the Eastern Orthodox Church.

The new leader of the Moscow school was Dionisii (1450–1508). Unlike his predecessors, he was not a monk but a lay painter who worked for the Palace of Arms in Moscow and for private patrons. With the growing sophistication of the age, Dionisii brought intellect to his art, rather than depending on an instinctive outpouring of spirituality.

Even so, he managed to emphasize the mystical over the dramatic in his narrative paintings. He elongated his figures, giving them a weightlessness, abandoned tight composition in favour of a processional effect and built subtle colour schemes of pale green, turquoise and rose against purple and dark blue.

Now that it headed the Orthodox world, the Russian Church sought to assert its authority. It laid down the rules of a new didactic iconography that was to explain the dogmas, rites and mysteries of the Church to the illiterate. The rules were drawn so tightly that they restricted the development of ecclesiastical iconography. Icons became smaller, cluttered, decorative and insipid.

▶ **The Holy Trinity**
Born in Moscow and trained in Trinity Monastery in Zagorsk, Andrei Rublev was the father of the famous Moscovite school, which came to dominate Russian icon painting some hundred years later (complete icon pictured opposite, detail shown on page 89)

overleaf ▶ **Transfiguration of Christ**
Theophanes the Greek was influential in the development of icon painting (detail shown on page 88, complete icon pictured on page 85)

overleaf ▶ **The Holy Trinity**
Rublev worked as Theophanes' assistant in 1405 on the Cathedral of the Annunciation. Despite this close association Rublev developed his style independently. Both men equalled each other in their mastery of their art (detail shown on page 89, complete icon pictured opposite)

However, in the sixteenth and seventeenth centuries private patronage began to play a growing role in the production of icons, and as a result the development of icon painting took a new and more fertile course. As Russia became more prosperous, wealthy merchants and landowners built private chapels and set up their own workshops to produce icons. The most famous was the Stroganov School in Perm, where the icons were made for the members of the Stroganov family of rich merchants who had an estate there.

These works usually bear the name of the person who commissioned them on the back. Many are small works that were not designed to hang on iconostases. Rather they were to be held in the hand and worshipped in private. They were extremely popular among the rich and the nobility.

Out of the control of the Church, these icons depended for their popularity solely on their richness and artistic quality. Muted colours, particularly rich, golden browns, dominated. Stroganov artists compensated with superb composition, which allowed numerous figures to appear on even the smallest icon without its appearing overcrowded.

The Church fathers had prohibited the use of naturalism, but the masters of the Stroganov School slipped naturalistic details into the

background. They used gold and silver lavishly in linear highlights and abstract patterns. Halos were made of beaten gold and icons were embellished with frames of precious metals. However, this ornamentation detracted from the spiritual significance of the icon. Eventually it overwhelmed the subject matter entirely and, in the mid-seventeenth century, the Stroganov School went into decline.

Until the seventeenth century, Russian icon painting resisted all Western influences. At this time, however, Tsar Michailovich (1645–76) imported Western artists to decorate his palaces. They inspired Simon Ushakov (1626–86), a silver-worker who was employed in the Tsar's armoury studio. He began painting icons that used the techniques that the Western artists brought with them. Although for his subject matter Ushakov stuck to the traditional canon, he incorporated perspective and modelled his figures using light and shade.

Ushakov's use of three-dimensional space and chiaroscuro was quickly copied by other icon painters. However, his techniques were condemned by the Church. His realistic approach, as opposed to the flat symbolism of

▲ ▶ St Nicholas surrounded by scenes from the life of Christ

In the sixteenth-century society, the Stroganov School in Perm became the most fashionable icon painters in Russia. The icons were unusual in that they were designed for individual and private worship (complete icon pictured opposite, details shown above)

traditional icons, was seen as blasphemy. This revived the old iconodule/iconoclast conflict. The portrayal of religious figures as real human beings was considered profane.

The Westernization of icons became even more of a threat when, in 1703, Tsar Peter I moved his capital westwards to St Petersburg. Mainstream art abandoned its Russian traditions and adopted the secular Western Baroque style. To counter this, Orthodox workshops were set up that concentrated on producing the old type of icons. They were highly disciplined and, in order that any hint of individuality could be rooted out, a production line was set up. Each step in the production – from preparing the wood to applying the varnish – was assigned to the person who was best at it.

In the first half of the nineteenth century, icons came under threat once again. The fashion for modernity meant that medieval icons were stripped from many of the larger Russian churches. This move was opposed by a sect called the Old Believers. Their zeal in preserving what they saw as precious religious artefacts attracted the attention of art lovers who began collecting icons for their aesthetic merit alone – thus saving many of the works that are now seen as the chief glory of medieval art.

The craze for modernism also put a lot of the icon painters out of work. Many moved to the wooded districts of Suzdal and Vladimir, settling in the villages of Mstera, Palekh and Shuya, where they formed themselves into guilds. There they turned out shoddy work in production-line fashion in a desperate attempt to keep their heads above water. However, the mass production of cheap, brightly coloured prints only served to reduce their income still further.

The twentieth century brought the Russian Revolution and the Communist authorities put a stop to icon production altogether. However, the better painters were drafted into workshops that turned out highly decorated lacquer boxes that were greatly prized throughout the Soviet era. This work preserved the techniques of the icon painters that had been handed down from father to son from the Middle Ages.

With the collapse of Communism the theft of icons from Russian churches and their illegal export to the West became big business. However, in the subsequent economic turmoil it has been hard to detect any revival in the production of religious icons.

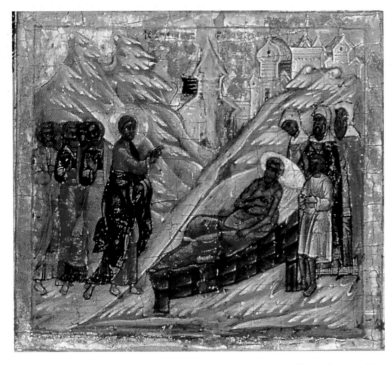

▲ ▶ **Christ the King**

The Stroganov School reached its zenith in the seventeenth century
(complete icon pictured opposite, detail shown above)

BIBLIOGRAPHY

Aidan, Brother, **Sacred Icons: Paradise Regained** (Newtown, Powys, 1991)

Anatoly of Kerch, Archbishop, **The Russian Icon** (The Anargyroi Press, Wallasey, 1994)

Brenske, Helmut, **Icons: Windows to Eternity** (Berghaus, Hannover, 1996)

Cassidy, Brendan (ed.), **Iconography at the Crossroads** (Princeton University Press, New Jersey, 1993)

Cavarnos, Constantine, **Byzantine Sacred Art** (The Institute for Byzantine and Modern Greek Studies, Inc., Belmont, Massachusetts, 1985)

Cormack, Rodin, **Painting the Soul: Icons, Death Masks and Shrouds** (Reakton Books, London, 1997)

Gennadios, Limouris (comp.), **Icons: Windows on Eternity** (WCC Publications, Geneva, 1990)

Grabar, André, **Christian Iconography: A Study of its Origins** (Routledge & Kegan Paul, London, 1969)

Jenkins, Simon, **Windows into Heaven: The Icons and Spirituality of Russia** (Lion Publishing, Oxford, 1998)

Minto, Marilyn, **Windows into Heaven: An Introduction to the Russian Icon** (Cardiff, 1996)

Onasch, Konrad, **Icons** (Faber & Faber, London, 1963)

Quenot, Michel, **The Icon: Window on the Kingdom** (Mowbray, London,1991)

Runciman, Steven, **Byzantine: Style and Civilization** (Penguin Books, London, 1990)

Talbot Rice, David, **Art of the Byzantine Era** (Thames and Hudson, London, 1994)

Talbot Rice, T., **Icons** (Studio Editions, London, 1990)

Taylor, John, **Icon Painting** (Phaidon Press, Oxford, 1979)

Temple, Richard, **Icons and the Mystical Origins of Christianity** (Element Books, Shaftsbury, 1990)

Weitzmann, Kurt, Chatzidakis, Manolis, Miatev, Krsto, Radojcic, Svetozar, **Icons from South Eastern Europe and Sinai** (Thames and Hudson, London, 1966)

Zaczek, Iain, **The Art of the Icon** (Studio Editions, London, 1994)

PICTURE ACKNOWLEDGEMENTS

AKG, London 6–7, 9, 11, 12–13, 16–17 Tracing, 24–25, 37 Background, 39 Left, 40, 48–49 Tracing, 50–51, 57, 64, 71, 76–77, 81, 87 /Byzantine Museum, Athens 41 /Archivio Cameraphoto Venezia 48 /Erich Lessing 19 Main Picture, 19 Centre Left, 23, 27, 29, 30, 31, 42, 43, 59 /Galerie der Matica Srpska 44–45 /National Museum, Ohrid, Macedonia 56 Top Right /Jean-Louis Nou 15 Top, 22 /Novi Sad, Galerie der Matica Srpska 62, 65 /Robert O'Dea 32–33 Tracing, 33 /Rome, Oratorio di S. Silvestro 34–35, /Rubljov Museum for Old Russian Art 38 /Mount Athos, Serbian Monastry of Hilandar 69 /Serbian Monastry of Hilandar 54 /Skopje, Art Gallery 53, 55 /Sofia, National Kunstgalerie 56 Bottom Left /Moscow, Tretjakov Gallery 84, 85, 88, 89
Bridgeman Art Library, London/New York/Museo Archeologico Nazionale, Naples, Italy 17 Right /Ashmolean Museum, Oxford, UK 17 Top Left, 17 Centre Left, 17 Bottom Left /Bargello, Florence, Italy 37 Centre /Private Collection 66, 72–73, 90 Top, 90 Centre, 91 /Hagia Sophia, Istanbul, Turkey Front Cover Background, 75 /Monastery of St Catherine, Mount Sinai, Egypt/Index 15 Bottom Left /Private Collection/Novosti 4–5, 78–79, 80–81 Tracing /Richardson and Kailas Icons, London, UK Front Cover left, Front Cover Right, Front Cover Centre, 82, 92, 93 /Cathedral of Santa Sofia, Ohrid, Macedonia 61 /Louvre, Paris, France/Peter Willi 16
Christies Images Ltd 2000, 21, 47, 83
Courtesy of Sotheby's Picture Library, London 39 Right